77 Tips
For A
Grown-Up Man

Kurt Starnes

Disclaimer: The author of this book is not a medical doctor, psychologist, psychiatrist, fitness instructor, chemist, nutritionist or holder of any other professional qualification. You should practice common sense and consider consulting with your own doctor or appropriate expert before attempting or applying some of the tips in this book.

To my daughter, Ellison,
All the stars in the sky are there for you.

CONTENTS

ACKNOWLEDGMENTS

This book is dedicated to my exceptionally brilliant daughter, whose mere presence has motivated me to improve myself and inspired me to gather my thoughts and express them on these pages. She has changed my life and enriched every moment, even now that she's almost a teenager. Thank you, Ellison.

To my mom, dad, grandmother and grandfather, who laid the foundation and provided the support I needed to take action and grow, I thank you and love you.

And to my other family members and friends, both online and off, who have supported me with kind words and encouragement, and some with editing, I send you all my most sincere thanks.

I would also like to give special recognition to Lisa Brandt Heckman and Lifehacker (lifehacker.com). Lisa posted a story from Lifehacker, "10 Things You Need To Do If You Were Just Fired," to Facebook, which inspired me to write. Had it not been for Lisa's post of the Lifehacker article, this book would probably not have been written.

PREFACE

Since I'm not a completely Grown-Up Man, the tips in this book touch on aspects of my life in which I think I've achieved Grown-Up Man status. It is not my intention to preach from these pages as I could probably learn a lot from you. And, just because a tip appears in this book doesn't mean I've permanently mastered it; many require constant discipline!

I've chosen these 77 tips because they've worked for me or are worthy goals. This list is neither definitive nor exhaustive and each tip may not apply to you. Scores of tips have been excluded because I considered them too obvious. Many included tips are general and stand on their own, while others are just starting points for further discussion or research.

These tips are drawn from my lifetime of ups and downs and from the people who were there along the way to give me a hand. I hope you find something in here that makes you think and motivates you to improve yourself. I endeavor to do my darndest to keep growing up and adding to this list.

INTRODUCTION

An important theme throughout the past several years of my life, and thus this book, is the sustainability of my actions. My qualifying question is, "Is it likely that I will maintain this action that I start today for most of the rest of my life?" My thoughts on diet and exercise especially reflect this theme of sustainability.

My general life philosophies are mostly derived from observing and listening to my parents and grandparents and experiencing the effect of their advice. They've typically been correct.

While my own parenting philosophies may be somewhat unproven — my daughter is just now almost a teenager — all signs appear to point to success. So far. My daughter's mom plays a critical role as well. Two loving parents who get along and share a deep, common love for the child, or children, is paramount. But, that's another book!

This book will be most helpful if:

You have access to a library or computer that you can use to delve deeper into some of the tips on this list;

You have read this book's disclaimer and know that I don't hold any kind of professional qualification;

You are smart enough not to do anything suggested in this book without reasonable thought and, if needed, consultation with a properly qualified professional or expert;

You know that nothing worthwhile comes quickly or easily; and

You would like to live a long, healthy and satisfying life.

1 EAT HEALTHY

Being healthy and fit won't eliminate life's struggles, but it will improve your ability to manage adversity. If you physically feel good, your outlook will improve and your brain will work better.

You don't need another diet book telling you what is healthy and what is junk food because you already know this. I'll make a few suggestions, but this chapter and book will not help you pick foods or plan your meals.

What you need to know is exactly how many calories you are consuming each day and the distribution of carbohydrate, fat and protein calories in your diet. You may think you're eating well, but until you log every item you consume you're just guessing.

1) Track your calories. Knowing your daily calorie count is absolutely necessary if you want to gain a meaningful understanding of your diet. Sites like Daily Burn (dailyburn.com) and Livestrong (livestrong.com) maintain large databases of grocery and restaurant foods that make it easy to find and log the foods you eat, and track your caloric intake as you go. While both sites offer premium, paid memberships, the features mentioned here are available with free memberships.

After an initial set-up, both sites will show your daily calories burned against daily calories consumed. A few months of food logging should educate you enough so that you can continue forward without the need to record every snack and meal. I do occasionally slip-up, so a refresher course in meal tracking helps get me back in line and adds some discipline to my routine.

Just knowing where I am in my calorie count helps me manage my intake. And here's a side-tip: don't let everyone know how many calories you just ate or the details of your diet plan unless they ask. This tip comes by way of someone advising me!

2) Track your carbohydrate, fat and protein intake. Before you change your diet, you need to understand the distribution of carbohydrate, protein and fat calories in the meals you eat. As you log your meals, both Daily Burn and Livestrong will chart this distribution on a daily basis.

When I first started logging meals, I was surprised to discover that I was getting well over 50% of my daily calories from carbohydrates, which is generally considered too much.

Don't obsess over some exact proportion, just keep it balanced in somewhat equal measures. I try to get about 40% of my calories from carbohydrates and 30% of calories from protein and fat respectively. This is a good, general rule, but you should conduct your own research or consider checking with a professional to see if your needs may be different.

Just as you'll learn about the calorie content of different foods by following tip No. 1, you'll also learn the carbohydrate, fat and protein calorie distribution in the foods you eat if you follow this tip.

After several days, take a look at your diet logs. Are you consuming many more calories than you are burning? Is one component of your carbohydrate, fat or protein consumption disproportionate from the others? If so, you already know what you need to do.

3) Get a small scale for your kitchen. This is an important tool for accurately weighing food items you need to log which are not already measured. I bought a digital postal scale at an office supply store, but you may already have a scale around your home. Don't worry, you won't need to weigh food for the rest of your life; after a few months your weight estimating skills will be more finely tuned.

4) Eat eggs. The seeds of animal life are rich in a broad spectrum of critical nutrients. Studies show that cholesterol in eggs does not translate to higher cholesterol in humans. I eat a couple of plain, boiled eggs a day for a low-calorie, protein rich morning snack.

(Search: health benefits of eggs)

5) Make and eat steel-cut oatmeal. Buy a can of the real deal, McCann's, read the directions and make it right. One cup of dry oats should yield about two pounds of cooked oats, or about four eight-ounce servings. Eat a serving and store the rest in the refrigerator. When you're ready for more, weigh out eight ounces of cooked oatmeal and a dash of water into a microwave safe cup or bowl and heat until warm. For healthy sweetening, I add a tablespoon of raw honey and a teaspoon of bee pollen per oatmeal serving.

Studies have found that eating oats is one of the most effective ways to lower cholesterol levels.

(Search: health benefits of oatmeal)

6) Take flax seed and/or fish oil. I've been taking omega-3 fatty acid supplements in the form of flax seed oil almost daily for over 20 years. At a minimum, I think this has improved and preserved the condition of my skin. While I believe the health benefits go well beyond this, I can't definitively say more. But, scientific studies have been verifying some of the historical claims regarding flax seed oil, including its ability to lower blood pressure and reduce the risk of heart disease, among other good things.

In addition to flax seed oil, you should also research fish oil, which is another excellent source of omega-3 fatty acids. Studies show that fish oil is superior to flax seed oil for supplying the omega-3 fatty acids EPA and DHA.

(Search: health benefits of flax seed oil and fish oil)

7) Eat flax seeds. All the benefits of flax seed oil plus the fiber. I buy it ground or cut, but not roasted. Add to yogurt, salads or smoothies for a nutty touch.

8) Eat bee pollen. It tastes awesome, is full of concentrated nutrition, may alleviate allergies if local pollen is consumed and is made by bees. Bees! Start with a grain or two and slowly work up to more if smaller amounts can be tolerated. I enjoy several teaspoons a day and have read, but haven't personally verified, that a human could survive on bee pollen alone. Use your search engine skills to learn more.

This is one of those items that you must be careful with if you have any bee related allergies. Please check with your doctor before proceeding.

(Search: health benefits of bee pollen)

2 GET FIT

You probably won't maintain an exercise regimen over many years if it's too complicated and takes too long. If you presently go to the gym and lift weights for three hours a day, will you maintain this routine for 10 or 20 years?

Because of my somewhat obsessive-compulsive personality that led to a cycle of intense workouts for months followed by periods of total inactivity, I had to create a fitness program that was quick, effective and sustainable. This program continues to work for me and it may work for you.

Quick means that each exercise tip can be completed in about 10 minutes and the walk or jog in 30 minutes. Effective means that each exercise works large muscle groups using your own body weight, ensuring natural, balanced muscle development and strength. Sustainable means that each day the exercises can be done wherever you are and done quickly — no gym, weights or specialized equipment is needed.

This is not a training program for a marathon or a body building tournament, but basic tips to employ for the rest of your life so that you'll look fit and feel good.

As you build stamina and get stronger, you may want to run farther and add new exercises to your routine. Go for it; just try to avoid creating an overly demanding and complex program that causes you to dread your next workout.

9) Pull up your body. Get a bar and hang it in a doorway you pass through many times a day. I hung one in the door between my room and bathroom. Start with just one pull-up. If you can only do one, then do that one and rest a full day before you make another go. Maybe you can only do one again, maybe two, but you will get stronger and be able to do more if you continue to do the exercises every other day. Keep this up until you can do at least five sets of one, with a one minute break in between each set.

Sustainable means doing no more than five sets every other day; each set doing as many as you can until you can't pull up your body again. This routine should take around 10 minutes and no more than 15, even if you're doing large numbers of repetitions. Remember, there's no hurry and this is not a competition.

Search the terms below to learn about different grips and the muscle groups they target. If you travel often, you could get a portable pull-up/chin-up bar, but don't worry if you miss a day or two, just don't let too much time pass between workouts.

(Search: pull-ups, chin-ups)

10) Push up your body. All you need for push-ups is yourself, gravity and the ground. Do five sets, each set as many as you can with one minute of rest in between sets. Do these every other day on the days you don't do pull-ups/chin-ups.

For proper form and to learn about different styles, search push-ups on YouTube. As you get stronger, you may want to get more creative.

Like pulling up your body, pushing up your body works large groups of muscles and should develop your upper body in a natural, balanced way using only your body weight as resistance.

11) Propel your body over land. Once again, just you, gravity and the ground are needed for this exercise. Start with 30 minute walks every other day and add some short jogs during the walks, but only when it feels comfortable. Your goal is a 30-minute jog every other day. If your plan is to only walk, then doing so daily is fine. Keep it fun and don't push yourself too much. You're not training for a marathon in six weeks; you're establishing a life-long program.

If you dread your next jog, walk instead. If you miss a few days, don't worry; just get back out as soon as you can. Consistency over many years is much more beneficial than brief streaks of intense activity in between long, sedentary periods.

As you get stronger and build stamina, you may want to run farther and faster. That's OK; just don't create a routine that becomes so strenuous that you dread your next outing. Slow and steady over many years will win the race!

12) Make your body like a board. This is called the plank hold and it's very good for strengthening the muscles of your torso.

Lie on your stomach with your shoulders propped-up above your elbows then raise and straighten your body from your feet to your shoulders while squeezing your abdominal and gluteal muscles. If this is too difficult, try it from your knees. The goal is to hold your body straight for as long as possible. There's also a variation doing this on your side, which instructions you'll find via the search terms below.

This exercise may be difficult, but try to work towards 60 to 90 seconds each set and do four to five sets with one minute of rest in between sets. Be sure to rest in between days.

(Search: ab plank hold and ab side bridge)

13) Learn good form running. A recent, famous Harvard study found that running barefoot or wearing shoes with minimal cushioning can diminish or eliminate heel strike, which lessens the impact of each stride, thus reducing the chance of running based injuries.

Since I learned the proper form, my running speed has increased fairly dramatically and I don't feel like I'm working any harder. While I have yet to run without shoes, I now use a minimal shoe.

(Search: harvard running study and good form running)

14) Get a six-pack. Not of beer, but of well-defined abdominal muscles. The six-pack is mostly the result of diet, not sit-ups, crunches or plank holds. Abdominal exercises will not spot reduce fat at your midsection. Focus on basic training, as outlined above, combined with a balanced, managed diet and your six-pack will emerge.

15) Check your BMI. The Body Mass Index simply looks at the relationship of your weight to your height. It's a very general measurement, but may be of some help in determining if you're carrying too much weight. You might think that a mirror would be enough to make such a determination, but, like me, you may need to see your BMI calculation to get the message.

(Search: bmi)

16) Check your blood pressure. If you're already getting regular physicals, you're covered. If not, take the next trip to the grocery or drug store and check your blood pressure. You've probably seen the machines at most stores near the pharmacy.

These machines shouldn't replace a doctor, but a self-administered check-up could provide a valuable warning if something is wrong.

17) Work towards a personal best in some activity or event. A record number of push-ups, the fastest time for a distance run or a waist size not seen in many years — do something you've never done before, or not done in many years. Such a personal best can be a very fulfilling accomplishment, especially if you can now outperform your teen or 20-something self.

Achievements in one part of your life can overflow into other parts and provide confidence and even inspiration.

3 TAKE CONTROL

I've struggled with addiction in various forms for a significant part of my life, but it was only after I overcame many of those addictions that I realized that addiction itself is a loss of self-control. What seems so profoundly obvious to me now was once hidden behind a wall of delusion. If only I had been able to see addiction as a weakness of character, I might have taken control of my life much sooner. If you suffer from an addiction or two, I hope that this perspective helps you retake control of your life.

18) Drink alcohol in moderation. Or don't drink it at all. Once you start logging calories and tracking your carbohydrate, protein and fat intake, you heavy drinkers might be surprised at how quickly your daily diet plan goes awry.

While there are studies which show that very moderate, daily consumption of alcohol may be beneficial to your health, regular, excessive drinking will make losing weight and keeping fit extremely difficult, if not impossible. Experience says that it will also create problems in your life well beyond your physical health.

(Search: diet fat alcohol)

19) Quit Nicotine. If you smoke or use other tobacco products, you may have started as an act of rebellion or independence. Nicotine can quickly take control and make you a helpless dependent, which is hardly a hallmark of a rebel. Maybe you have the personality type that allows you to decide when you want to smoke, but for most folks, including me at one time, the craving for nicotine decides.

I can recall needing to light up when I didn't want to or making a cigarette run at odd hours when I would have rather stayed at home.

I quit with the help of nicotine gum, and it was still quite difficult. Whatever method you choose, take action and quit now. I've never met a person who regretted quitting cigarettes or tobacco products.

20) Quit drugs. Just like nicotine addiction, drug dependency represents a personal loss of control. All of the rationalizations you can muster will not justify regular drug use. You know what kind of drugs I'm talking about. If you're using something daily, you must quit. Reality is not improved on drugs and you are likely not more productive and creative on drugs.

You may be able to refer to a great artist, musician or writer who created a masterpiece while high, but for every one of those there are likely millions who exist or died in obscurity. Human senses are highly evolved and almost always function best unhindered.

Decide to take control and quit. Get started today at the top of this list with health and fitness and seek professional help if needed.

21) Enjoy chocolate and sweets? I'm tempted to say don't worry about this vice if you've got the above three under control, but like everything else, moderation applies. The good news is that my research and personal experience show that you can splurge on treats one day a week, as long as you are otherwise consistently eating well and exercising.

4 LOOK SHARP

These next tips have nothing to do with being a metrosexual. They're about basic male hygiene and taking pride in your appearance. Since when was not taking care of yourself considered manly?

22) Use a washcloth or exfoliating soap. I grew up using soap and a wash cloth in the bath or shower, but somewhere along the way I switched to just a bar of soap. From talking to other folks, this seems like a trend among Generation X, perhaps based on a need for quicker showers.

Humans are constantly shedding skin, so when you bathe use a washcloth or some liquid exfoliating soap. There's even exfoliating bar soap. This bathing practice will slough off dead skin cells, help to unblock pores, aid circulation and just make you feel better.

23) Moisturize your face. If you regularly take an omega-3 supplement like fish or flax oil, you may already enjoy the natural suppleness such oils can bring to your skin from the inside. But, you may also need some extra help from the outside. I use a daily moisturizer with sunscreen and apply it after every shower.

There are now some excellent men's facial moisturizers available at your local market or pharmacy; you'll likely find them in the shaving products section. For natural or higher-end men's products, visit one of the large beauty supply chains or department store cosmetic counters.

24) Manage thy nose and ear hairs. While thick nests of ear and nostril hair may have proven beneficial to your distant ancestors, these protruding tufts are now frightening to loved ones, friends and children.

End the horror and get yourself some ear and nose hair clippers. It was a difficult purchase for me as it was an admission that I was getting old, but don't resist.

25) Keep your fingernails and toenails trimmed and neat. Whether you do this yourself or get a manicure and pedicure, it will improve your appearance and self-esteem and will make a good impression on those around you. Well-kept nails and cuticles are signs of calmness and self-control.

I have a history of nail biting and cuticle picking, so this is one of those tips I still struggle with.

26) Use moist toilet wipes. Yes, this is a personal one and there's no need for me to go into fine detail. If you want to be properly clean, follow this tip.

5 LEARN SOMETHING

While children and young adults are formally charged with learning, us grown-ups sometimes ease up on daily education. With most of civilization's collective knowledge at your fingertips, it's an injustice to let even a single day pass without learning at least one thing, regardless of your age.

27) Listen. Especially to folks older than you. While there is merit to learning by screwing-up, there's also some serious positive reinforcement to be gained from experiencing good advice work!

28) Use your smart phone to get smart. Silently reading and tapping out text on your mobile phone at a lunch table or social event is rude and unacceptable. Consulting a search engine to find the answer to an interesting question or to remember a fleeting fact is acceptable, should be encouraged and can be fun!

Back in school, I was told that if I came upon a word that I didn't understand, I should look it up in a dictionary. That rule has been modernized, extended and expanded for the networked age. If you come across a word, subject, event or anything you don't understand or know about, search it on the Web.

29) Learn how to perform an effective web search. The information you need is probably on the Internet, but it's of no use if you can't find it. My daughter and I play a mobile phone game to see who can grab the information we seek with the simplest, quickest search. It's fun and constructive. I think this trial and error method is the best way to learn how to do a good search.

As you have seen, I sometimes add a few search terms after certain tips to aid your further research. You may have noted that I don't capitalize words that should be capitalized. Most search engines ignore caps and punctuation, so an efficient search can also ignore such formatting.

My favorite tool for an effective search is the exact phrase search, where the search terms are placed in the correct order within quotation marks. For example, a search for the terms *77 tips* without quotes returns 197 million hits on Google. Google is returning every webpage where both of these terms appear anywhere and in any order on those webpages. But, if I place the search terms in quotation marks, *"77 tips,"* then Google only returns 126,000 hits. Google is only returning websites where the search terms are adjacent and in the same order as my search terms in quotes. This can be a huge help and can be made even more powerful when used with additional search terms outside of the quotes, like *"77 tips" grown-up*, which is how you might search for this book.

(Search: effective search techniques)

30) Consult Wikipedia. Like any other encyclopedia, the information at Wikipedia is only as good as its sources. Pay close attention to the veracity of the references at the bottom of each subject page and follow the links for more detailed information. Wikipedia can be an outstanding place to start any quest for knowledge, just don't make it your only source.

31) Take a free class. Stanford and MIT are just two of many universities offering everything from individual lectures to full, free online courses. iTunes U also offers a broad selection of university classes and material including films and audiobooks. Finally, check out The Khan Academy, which offers over 2,000 video lessons and a goal to provide an outstanding and free education to anyone.

The amount of free educational material online is so vast that entire books are probably devoted to this one subject. Your favorite search engine is the best tool for finding free courses that interest you the most.

(Search: free mit, free stanford, khan academy and itunes u)

32) Consult YouTube instructional videos. For almost anything you may want to learn how to do, there is at least one video on YouTube showing you exactly how to do it. Instruction on cooking, gymnastics, exercise, driving, yoga and many more subjects await you.

33) Know the exact time you were born. Your birth time should be right on the face of your birth certificate. I'm amazed at how few of my family and friends know this about themselves.

First light for me was at 3:43 p.m. on September 1, 1966.

34) Know your blood type. If you don't know your blood type, call your doctor and find out. It's your body and you never know when this information might save your life.

I'm A+.

35) Know your DNA. Since I haven't had a DNA screening yet, I'll wait for the next edition of this book to provide you with a firsthand account. I recommend that you consult a search engine or someone more familiar with the process if you'd like to learn more.

While it may seem frightening to learn that you might have a predisposition to a certain disease or condition, advance notice may provide you with an opportunity to treat and mitigate potential threats.

36) Learn about our planet and our neighborhood. On a cosmological scale our Solar System is a tiny, intimate place, so it's important to know some very basic facts about it.

You should know the distance from the Earth to the Sun and why we have seasons.

You should know the distance around the Equator.

You should know how long it takes the Earth to orbit the Sun. You did know that the Earth orbits the Sun, right?

You should know all of the planets in the Solar System in order, starting nearest the Sun.

And to better understand the Universe, you should know the speed of light.

6 THINK

Just before my 40th year, I began to more closely examine my personal political and religious beliefs. I also began to take a closer look at the many philosophical schools of thought. Your path will likely be different than mine, but I think the process of introspection and curiosity among middle-aged and older folks regarding such subjects is quite common and very important.

37) Challenge your beliefs, study what you oppose. Whatever your political, religious or philosophical beliefs are, make an effort to study and understand systems you might presently disagree with. It can be enlightening to find points that you agree with in belief systems that you thought you were totally against.

There are a lot of very smart folks who have different beliefs than you — don't shun them, embrace them.

38) Be non-partisan. Partisanship is the lens that allows you to find the flaws in the other party's candidate that you overlook in your party's candidate. If you spend a lot of time expressing your displeasure at only one party, you're partisan and not digging deep enough.

If you can quickly and definitively state your political affiliation, you probably don't know enough about the various political belief systems. Open your Internet and learn. I've only recently discovered that my political beliefs run across many different political schools. I bet yours do, too.

39) Keep an open mind. An open mind doesn't mean that you will believe everything you see, read and are told; it simply means that you won't summarily prejudge anything. In fact, an open mind is emblematic of a skeptic. Only after examining the evidence and learning more will you be closer to an opinion or judgment.

40) Know the limits of your knowledge. Before large online social networks, when folks spent most of their time conversing in small groups, you might have been able to play loose with the facts. No more. With potentially hundreds, thousands or even more reading your words daily, the chances of being tripped-up and even dressed-down by a scholar are greater than ever. Be careful.

It's OK if you don't know everything. When questioned, don't be afraid of answering, "I don't know" — it's a popular reply among smart folks.

41) Be positive. Your opinion about something says more about you than the subject of your opinion.

42) Appreciate your place. Occasionally take a moment to try to comprehend exactly where you are in the Universe: On a very small planet in an unimaginably immense space, where the unit of measurement is the distance that light travels in a year.

7 BE A GREAT DAD

If you don't yet have children, then now is the best time to read the below tips. I highly recommend kids, but only if you are willing to contribute a significant portion of your time to their upbringing. Being a dad is not easy, but it's the most satisfying job I've ever had.

What follows is a philosophy I've developed while raising my daughter, blended with the best lessons taught by my parents and grandparents. I think most of these tips would also apply to a son, but you probably don't need to be a gentleman and get your boy's door.

43) Make your mistakes teachable moments. Set an example for your children not as a perfect god, but as an imperfect human just like them. You will not be able to hide your mistakes, so highlight your failures and present them as endearing lessons on what not to do. This will create an environment of open dialog in which your kids will be more likely to admit and share their mistakes with you, but before they do, see Tip No. 55!

44) Your actions teach louder than your words. If you panic when you see a spider in your home, your kids will do the same. Further, their reaction to a cut or scrape they receive may be more based on your reaction than their pain. Your kids are watching everything you do and learning directly from your actions, and learning much less from your words. Don't underestimate this or their ability to pick up and copy the finest details of your behavior.

45) Discipline without anger. Being mad at your child is not a form of discipline. Calmly, even lovingly, deliver strong, appropriate punishment. Your child is more likely to change and grow from losing an important privilege than from you venting anger and frustration at them.

46) Apologize. Parents make mistakes, too, and when you do it is very important to apologize to your child promptly and sincerely. You should do this not only because it's proper, but also because you want your kids to express the same behavior when they screw up.

47) Be honest with your children. Don't trick your kids into eating right or behaving properly. Eating cookie dough does not cause worms and the Boogie Man will not get them for misbehaving. Be honest and explain why some foods are unhealthy and why certain behavior is unacceptable. They'll probably forgive you for tricking them about the Tooth Fairy, Easter Bunny and Santa Claus.

48) Be a mom. If you're married with kids and play the traditional working dad, take a week off from work, send your wife on a vacation and you take care of the kids. Do everything your wife does: cook meals, do laundry, manage the household and wrangle the kids. After playing mom, your respect for your wife will have increased dramatically and you'll be ready for some relative relaxation back at work.

49) Always get the door for a lady, even if she's your own daughter. The example will not be soon forgotten and may ensure that she falls in love with a gentleman.

50) Spend time with your children. You may not know it yet, but you likely need them more than they need you. No gift you can give your children is more valuable than your time.

51) Stay neutral. Teach your kids how to think, learn and analyze for themselves. You should resist the urge to indoctrinate them into your belief systems. Be a strong example of what is right and mete out firm discipline when appropriate, but allow your kids to decide important issues for themselves at the appropriate time.

As a parent, you have tremendous power to shape their young minds. Don't program them; present a fair view of both sides of every issue. You may let them know how you feel, but also tell them that reasonable people may disagree with your position. This exercise can be helpful to both you and your kids.

52) Practice and preach the Golden Rule. My daughter has asked me many difficult questions about how to act in certain situations and the Golden Rule almost always applies. It can even be applied in your relationship with your children.

Entire self-help books on parenting, relationships and even business are rendered virtually unnecessary with this simple maxim.

53) Free your children. Of course you must consider the amount of freedom to give them based on their age and responsibility level, but fight the natural tendency to try to protect them from all potential evil. They will eventually be on their own and an overprotective upbringing could make their struggle for independence much more difficult.

54) Don't move your child to a different class. It eventually happens to every kid; they learn that they are in the class of the claimed worst or grouchiest teacher. Unless there is some serious misconduct by the teacher, issues like this are to be handled between you and your child, not you and the school.

It is your responsibility to tell your child that life is not always fair and that he or she must make the best of a less than ideal situation. This is critical preparation for your child's future.

55) Keep communication open. Don't act surprised, get mad or be overly sensitive when your kids share a mistake they made or something personal with you. Try to manage your emotions when they tell you things that are unexpected. The tone of your voice and your reaction will determine to what degree they choose to share with you in the future.

Teach your kids tact, but don't create an environment that muzzles them and insulates you from things you don't want to hear.

8 BEHAVE

This chapter could go on for pages, so I've just chosen the items that have been the most meaningful in my life. Many of these tips are expressly the result of the patience and guidance shown to me by the folks who have loved me the most.

56) Be a gentleman. A gentleman is more than a veneer of good manners: he's unselfish, dependable, honest and loyal.

57) Forgive. I can't say it any more simply and more profoundly than Lily Tomlin: "Forgiveness means giving up all hope for a better past."

58) Always be kind. Every person you come across each day is struggling with something. Keep this in mind and be kind, even if the person you smile upon does not smile on you.

59) Don't get angry. Nothing good ever comes from anger; solutions are found by deliberate action. Not only is anger ineffective, it can damage feelings and harm relationships. Don't be passive; transform your anger into positive, constructive action.

60) Reserve the curse words. These powerful and often offensive words should be considered the nuclear option of your vocabulary. Instead of striking all curse words from your lexicon, give them purpose and save them for the rare moments when maximum impact is required or when genuine distress needs to be expressed.

It may surprise you, but this is the same advice I give to my young daughter.

61) Be credible. If you say you'll do it, do it. The quickest way to begin rebuilding credibility is to immediately commit to nothing, then work forward from there, one kept promise at a time.

62) Avoid hypocrisy. There's an innocent form of hypocrisy that I think is just part of human nature; one day I'm complaining to myself about the guy at the market with more than 15 items in the express lane and on another day I'm that guy. Since it's likely a universal trait, we're all experts at spotting it and calling it out. I've found that young children are especially sharp at recognizing such behavioral inconsistencies.

Hypocrisy is something that you should be sensitive to and try to avoid as it can eventually undermine your credibility.

63) The thought counts. It's perfectly acceptable to thank someone via a thoughtful email message, but if your old-school manners say otherwise, then mail a paper note. A personal thank you in any form is always better than nothing.

64) Choose your words carefully. While this is true for daily conversation and correspondence, it's especially valid for online activity. Assume that everything you post on the Internet will be viewed and read by everyone you know. And everyone you don't know.

Remember that once something is posted online, it could be archived via cache and made available forever, even if you delete the original.

65) Use your real name online. Don't use a handle or made-up name; identify yourself and stand by your words.

66) Be humble. There's no valid reason to think you're inherently better than anyone else, so why act that way? In my experience, arrogance is typically a function of insecurity or an unbroken run of success. Or both. If you've never failed, you're lucky, not smart.

67) Be a friendly and courteous driver. I am certain that world peace will not be achieved until every driver embraces this tip and exercises some simple courtesy on the road. What dumbfounds me is the rudeness of some drivers who, at some time, must have been saved by the kindness of a friendly driver.

9 LOOK BACK

Your distant memories may fade as you get older, but they can be brightened by a picture, song or seeing the name of an old friend. Such simple remembrances can light up once dark regions of your brain and initiate a cascade of activity that can expose very deep, linked memories. Revealing these hidden memories can be an extremely gratifying experience.

68) Map every house in which you've lived. Go to *Google Maps* and create a new map in *My Maps*. Start the search with just a click on the map in the general area of the home then readjust the cursor before the next click. I like the satellite view because sometimes landmarks like lakes and parks help me find the target home. When found, drop a pin on the roof and add a description. Continue to the next home, repeat until complete.

If Google has photographed the locations of your homes, you will be able to go to *Street View* and virtually travel up and down the streets of your old neighborhoods. This can be a deeply moving and powerful experience.

(Search: google my maps and street view)

69) Get back in touch with old friends online. I can't overstate how much it has meant for me to reunite with old friends via the Internet. It's not the same as being there, but regular online contact and interaction with the folks you've bonded with throughout your life is a meaningful way to keep the memory storage regions of your brain active. I've also become good friends with classmates who were once just acquaintances. I can't ever imagine going back to the time before I connected with so many people.

There are many communities online, but the place where you'll likely find most of your old friends is Facebook.

70) Save and review your old photos. And films, too. These are the lifelines to your memories and probably the strongest links to your past. Spend some time reviewing your historic photos and consider digitizing then archiving them online, if you haven't already done so.

10 LOOK AHEAD

There should be no day that marks the end of your productive life, when your work is finished and you decide you're going to sit in the sun and pass time. Instead, sit in the sun and plan your next big thing. There's never been a time when individuals were so empowered. Don't let it pass you by.

71) Hear. If your ability to hear is diminishing, seriously consider getting a hearing aid. Your inability to hear well not only handicaps you, but it creates an uncomfortable environment for the folks who'd like to converse with you. You also might miss something important.

You're not an old man, but a new cyborg. Humanity is entering an age when devices that can amplify and sharpen senses will probably become more common, even for folks with perfectly functioning senses. I expect that the generation brought up on Walkmans and iPods will inspire a hot new market of cool, high-tech hearing amplifiers.

72) See. If you've passed 40 and still don't need reading glasses, you're lucky. If you are around 40 and need to hold books and phones at arm's length to read, you're normal and need reading glasses.

Whether it's glasses, contacts or a surgical procedure, take action and sharpen your vision. There's just too much cool stuff you need to see.

73) Take pictures. If you have a mobile phone with a camera, make a habit of taking pictures. If you don't have a mobile phone, get an inexpensive pocket camera or disposable and keep it handy. You don't need a fancy camera and you don't have to wait for special events to take memorable photographs. Some of my favorite images are not technically outstanding and are probably not very interesting to anyone except me.

Remember, you're not just shooting pictures for yourself, but for your progeny to enjoy at some distant time in the future. Give them something to talk about.

74) Go first. Some say to follow the pioneers and learn from their mistakes. Nonsense. Start now, lead and learn from your own mistakes.

75) Set a goal to never quit setting goals. Each day is an opportunity to do something you've never done before or start working towards something you've never achieved. Always be working towards something, no matter how small.

76) These are the good old days. By almost every measure, us humans have never had it so good. There are no excuses; this is your time.

77) Write a book. Everyone has valuable knowledge to share once the thoughts are allowed to flow from the heart and mind. There's no financial barrier and there's no old-school publisher standing in your way. The book business has been democratized and publishing is now only a choice. Decide to share. Decide to write.

78) Don't grow up too much. This 78th tip is, perhaps, the most important one of all. It came to me after I had originally finished and published this book, so it doesn't appear in the earliest electronic versions. It's not even accounted for in the title!

There was a time when I dreamed of being a garbage man, riding on the back bumper of the truck between stops, wind in my face. When I was told that this job would probably require a daily bath, I decided that I'd rather be a superhero — a much cleaner endeavor, I thought. I didn't worry about how I'd become a superhero or whether I might fail, I just wanted to fly and wear a cape.

Growing up, I was taught that people don't fly or have magical powers, so I needed to choose a more practical profession. I became more aware of my limitations and more averse to failure. I was growing up too much.

It wasn't until after my own child was born that I began to experience life as a kid again, through my daughter's eyes. She wanted to be a princess and thought she could read my mind. The former is quite possible and the latter is now becoming science, with the help of sensors and computers. Yesterday's magic is today's reality — a very good reason not to discourage a child's dreams or limit your own.

While this book offers tips for grown-up men, this book's existence is symbolic of the fearlessness of youth, taking a chance and not growing up too much.

CONFESSIONS

Writing and publishing this book scared the heck out of me. My greatest fears were that the book wouldn't be long enough and that my writing wouldn't be good enough. I had to remind myself that this work might never be perfect, but it would have to get finished. I had to push forward, keep writing, continue editing, stick to my schedule and then force myself to stop proofreading and stop editing!

My daughter was observing my progress, so a failure to follow through would have been contrary to almost everything I've taught her.

About a week from my deadline, I found my voice and my insecurities began to fade. This little book may be too short and my writing may not be good enough, but I overcame my fears, gave it my very best and published.

Now, I only hope you've found something meaningful or inspiring here.

ABOUT THE AUTHOR

Kurt Starnes is a single dad, born in Texas and living in Southern California. Writing is his painful pleasure.

Kurt sometimes writes at his blog and enjoys sharing and discussing interesting items on Facebook, Twitter and Google Buzz about science, technology, photography and alternative music. Kurt is a skeptic with geek tendencies and has great optimism regarding the future. Prompted by his daughter, one of his simple goals each day of the last few years has been to "Learn something new today," which saying has become the tagline of his personal blog.